MDERN
WEDDING SONGS

T0039542

ISBN 978-1-5400-1397-2

HAL•LEONARD®
7777 W. BLUEMOUND RD. P.O. BOX 13819 MILWAUKEE, WI 53213

Visit Hal Leonard Online at
www.halleonard.com

ALL OF ME

Words and Music by JOHN STEPHENS
and TOBY GAD

ARE YOU GONNA KISS ME OR NOT

Words and Music by JIM COLLINS
and DAVID LEE MURPHY

Moderately, in 2

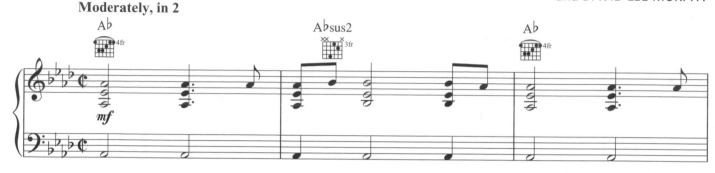

We were sit-tin' up there on your ma-ma's roof,
best ___ dang kiss that I ev-er had, ex-

talk-in' 'bout ev-'ry-thing un-der the moon. ___ With the
cept for that long ___ one af - ter that. ___ And I

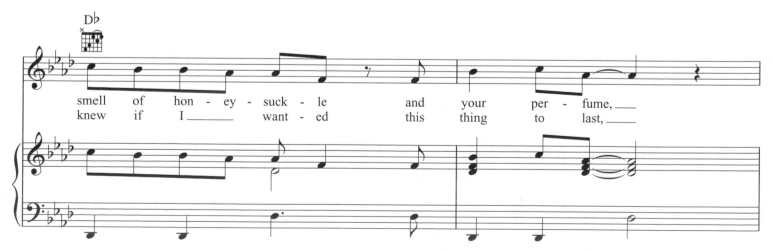

smell of hon-ey-suck-le and your per-fume, ___
knew if I ___ want - ed this thing to last, ___

all I could think a-bout was my next move. Oh, but
soon - er or lat - er I'd___ have to ask Oh for___

Eb

you were so shy; so was I.___ May-be that's why it was
your___ hand. So, I took a chance, bought a wed-din' band and I

Db

so hard to___ be - lieve___ when you smiled and said___ to me,___
got down on___ one knee.___ And you smiled and said___ to me,___

Eb   N.C.

___ "Are you gon - na kiss me or not?
___ "Are you gon - na kiss me or not?

you walked down the aisle.

When the preach-er man said, "Say I do," I did, and you did, too. Then I lift-ed that veil, saw your pret-ty smile, and I said, "Are you gon-na

CAN'T STOP THE FEELING

from TROLLS

Words and Music by JUSTIN TIMBERLAKE,
MAX MARTIN and SHELLBACK

Moderate Funk groove

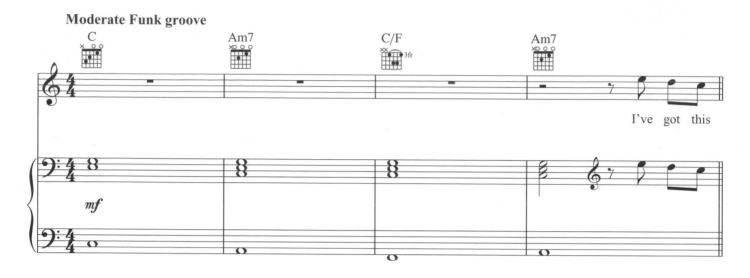

I've got this

feel-ing   in-side my bones.   It goes e - lec-tric, wav-y when I turn it
Ooh,   it's some-thing mag - i - cal.   It's in the   air, it's in my blood, it's rush-ing

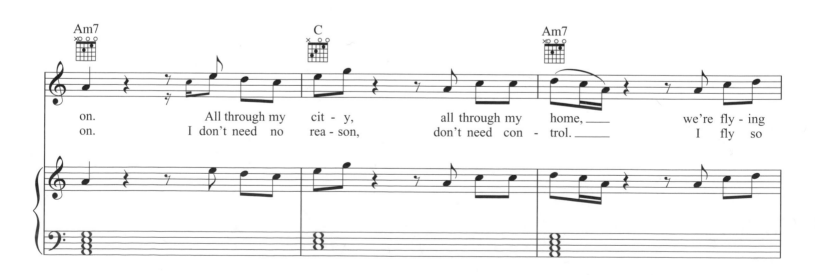

on.   All through my   cit - y,   all through my   home, ___   we're fly - ing
on.   I don't need no   rea - son,   don't need con - trol. ___   I fly so

EVEN MORE MINE
from MY BIG FAT GREEK WEDDING 2

Words and Music by NATHAN CHAPMAN,
RITA WILSON and DARRELL BROWN

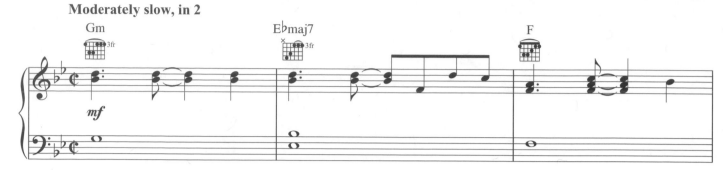

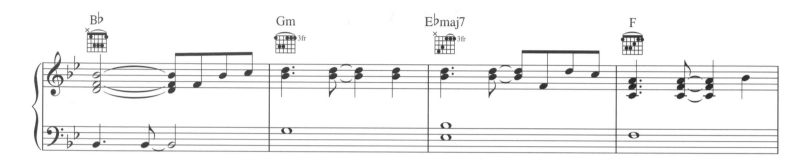

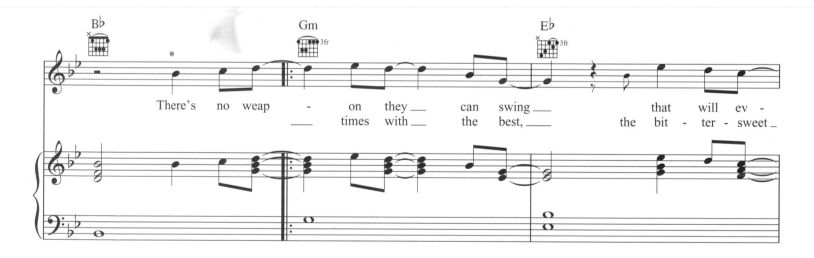

There's no weap - on they ___ can swing ___ that will ev - er
___ times with ___ can the best, ___ the bit - ter - sweet ___

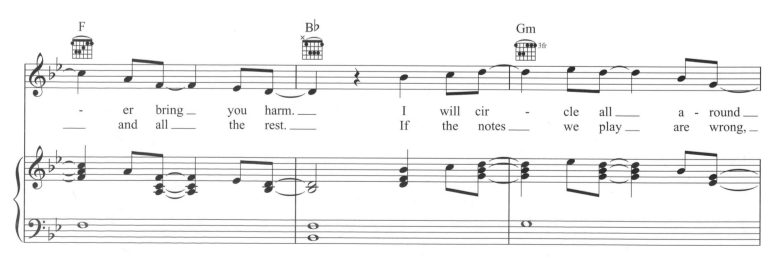

- er bring ___ you harm. ___ I will cir - cle all ___ a - round ___
___ and all ___ the rest. ___ If the notes ___ we play ___ are wrong, ___

* *Vocal sung an octave lower than written.*

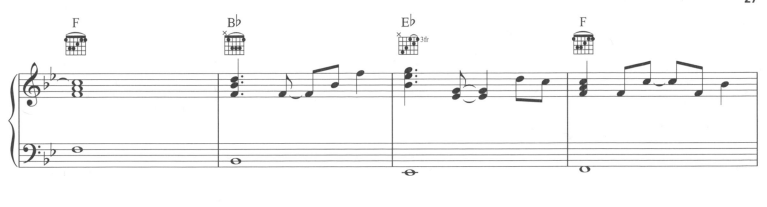

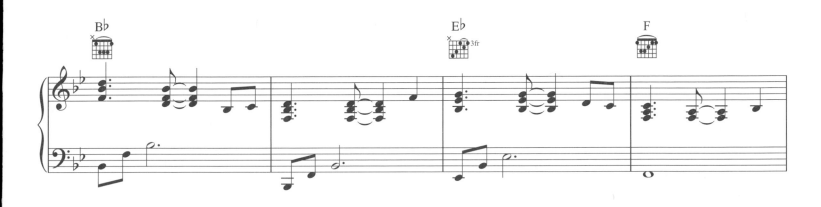

When you break ___ it down, ___ it's sim - ple: we are one ___

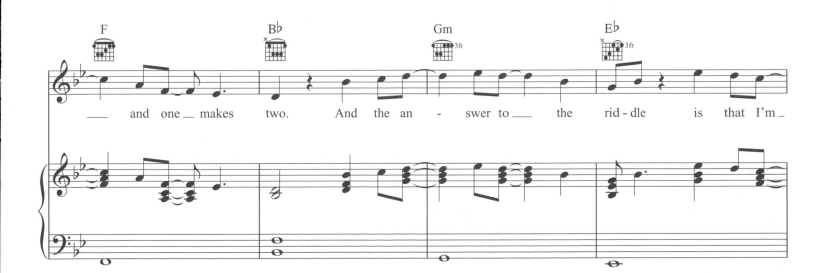

___ and one ___ makes two. And the an - swer to ___ the rid - dle is that I'm ___

FRESH EYES

Words and Music by ANDY GRAMMER,
IAN KIRKPATRICK and ROSS GOLAN

D.S. al Coda

-ment. If I could bot-tle this up, I would. _

CODA

eyes. _____ Ooh, _____

ooh. _____ Ooh. _____

FROM THE GROUND UP

Words and Music by DAN SMYERS,
SHAY MOONEY and CHRIS DESTEFANO

I CAN'T WAIT
(Be My Wife)

Words and Music by JAMES BAILEY,
RYAN OGREN, JON BERRY,
PETER MUNTERS and JAMES ULRICH

Moderate Country feel

The way you curse _ while we're _ in traf-fic, the mil-lion fla-vors of _ your chap-stick, the way that you _ keep my _ heart cap-tive.

Recorded a half step lower.

The Jour-ney con-cert in __ A - Z; re-

mem-ber, we __ sang "Faith - ful - ly"? __ I've still got __ that old __ ho-tel __ room

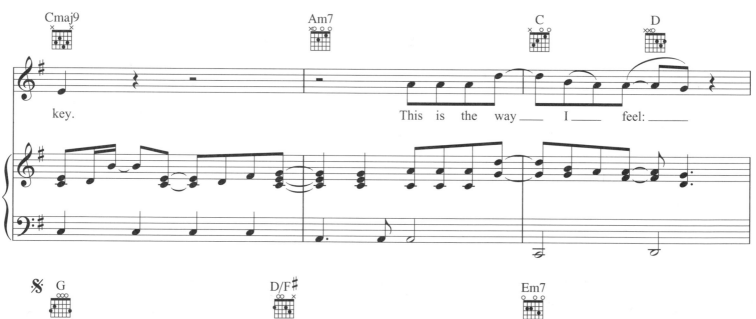

key.   This is the way __ I __ feel: _____

I can't wait for you _____ to be my wife, _____ to live this life __

I CHOOSE YOU

Words and Music by SARA BAREILLES,
PETER HARPER and JASON BLYNN

I DON'T DANCE

Words and Music by LEE BRICE,
DALLAS DAVIDSON and ROBERT HENRY HATCH JR.

Recorded a half step higher.

I GET TO LOVE YOU

Words and Music by MAGGIE ECKFORD
and MATT BRONLEEWE

Gently, in a slow 2

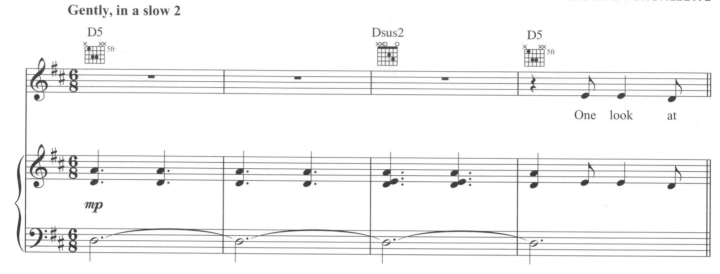

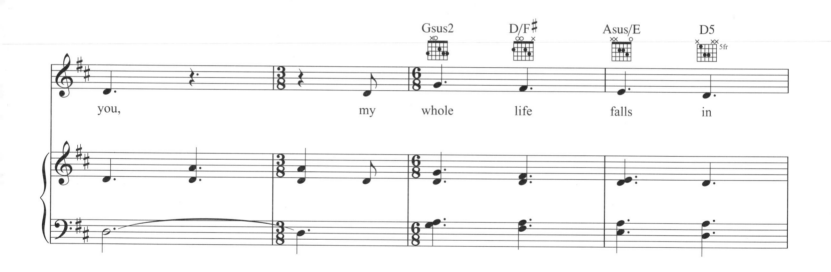

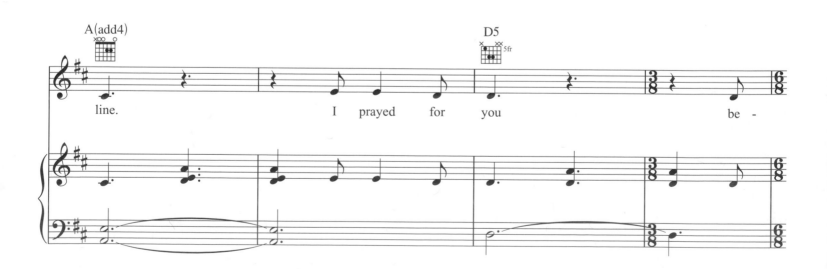

LOVE SOMEONE

Words and Music by JASON MRAZ, BECKY GEBHARDT,
MAI SUNSHINE BLOOMFIELD, CHASKA POTTER,
MONA TAVAKOLI, CHRIS KEUP
and STEWART MYERS

MARRY ME

Words and Music by DAVID KATZ,
PAT MONAHAN and SAM HOLLANDER

OLD FASHIONED

Words and Music by THOMAS CALLAWAY,
ALAN KASIRYE, RAEFORD GERALD
and JOE SIMON

MARRY YOU

Words and Music by BRUNO MARS,
ARI LEVINE and PHILIP LAWRENCE

Moderately fast

OVER AND OVER AGAIN

Words and Music by HELEN CULVER,
HARMONY SAMUELS, NATHAN SYKES
and MAJOR JOHNSON

MY VALENTINE

Words and Music by
PAUL McCARTNEY

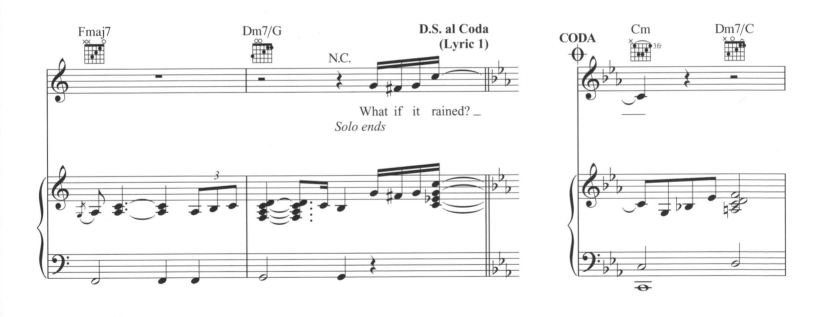

What if it rained? _
Solo ends

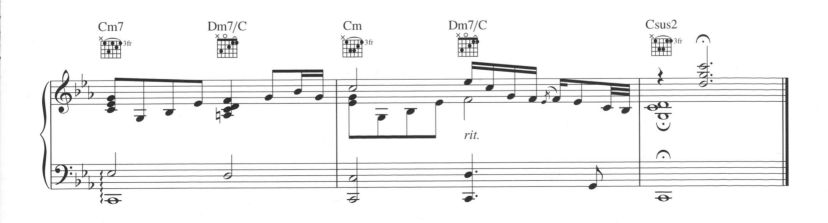

rit.

PERFECT

Words and Music by
ED SHEERAN

PLAY THAT SONG

Words and Music by HOAGY CARMICHAEL,
FRANK LOESSER, PAT MONAHAN
and WILLIAM WIIK LARSEN

RATHER BE

Words and Music by GRACE CHATTO,
JACK PATTERSON, NICOLE MARSHALL
and JAMES NAPIER

Recorded a half step lower.

Yeah, y - yeah, y - yeah, y - yeah, y - yeah, yeah, yeah.

When I ___ am with you, ___ there's no place ___ I'd rath-er be. ___

SAY YOU WON'T LET GO

Words and Music by STEVEN SOLOMON,
JAMES ARTHUR and NEIL ORMANDY

Moderate Ballad

I met you in the dark, you lit me up,
I wake you up with some break-fast in bed,

you made me feel as though I was e-nough.
I'll bring you cof-fee with a kiss on your head.
We danced the night a-way,
And I'll take the kids to school,

I knew I loved you then, but you'd nev - er know, 'cause I played it cool when I was
I'm so in love with you, and I hope you know, dar - ling, your love is more than
I'm gon - na love you till my lungs give out, I prom - ise till death we part

scared of let - ting go. _____ I know I need - ed you, but I nev - er showed,
worth its weight in gold. _____ We've come so far, my dear, look how we've grown,
like in our vows. _____ So I wrote this song for you, now ev - 'ry - bod - y knows

but I wan - na stay with you un - til we're gray and old. _____
and I wan - na stay with you un - til we're gray and old. _____ Just say you _ won't let go. _
that it's just you and me un - til we're gray and old. _____

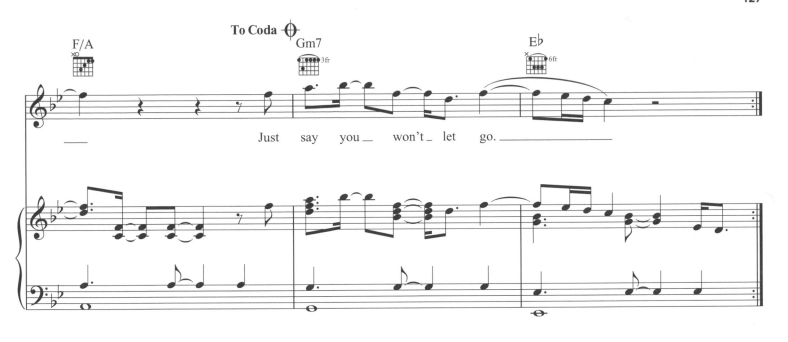

Just say you __ won't __ let go. _____

I wan-na live with you e-ven when we're ghosts, __

'cause you were al-ways there for me when I need-ed you most. _____

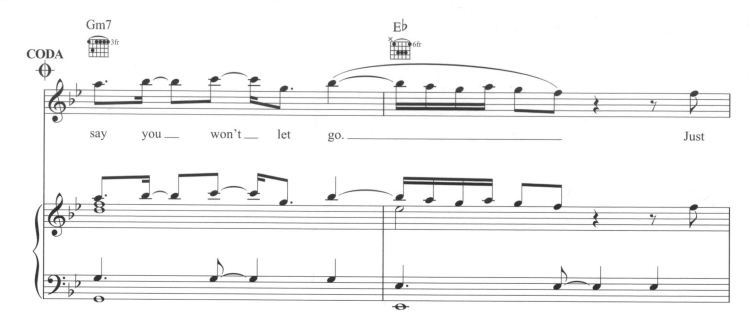

SOMETHING JUST LIKE THIS

Words and Music by ANDREW TAGGART,
CHRIS MARTIN, GUY BERRYMAN,
JONNY BUCKLAND and WILL CHAMPION

Oh, I want some-thing just like —

— this.

THINKING OUT LOUD

Words and Music by ED SHEERAN
and AMY WADGE

YOURS

Words and Music by RUSSELL DICKERSON,
CASEY BROWN and PARKER WELLING

Country Pop beat, in 2

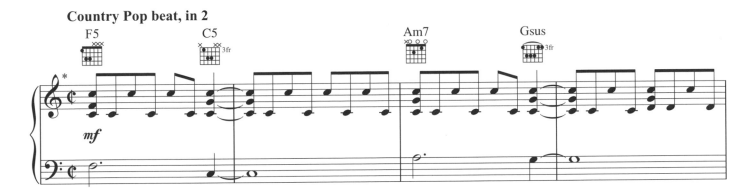

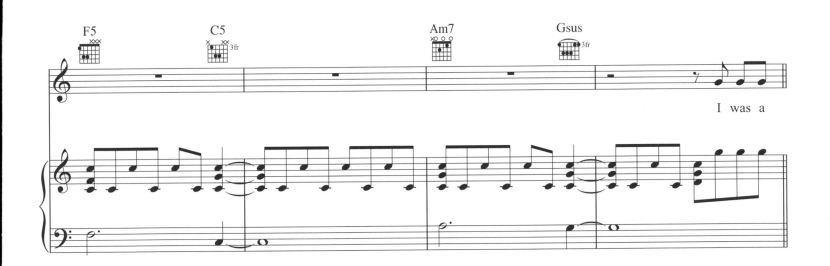

I was a

boat stuck in a bot-tle that nev-er got the chance to touch the sea; just for-

* *Recorded a half step lower.*

A THOUSAND YEARS

from the Summit Entertainment film THE TWILIGHT SAGA: BREAKING DAWN – PART 1

Words and Music by DAVID HODGES
and CHRISTINA PERRI

WHY I LOVE YOU

Words and Music by HARMONY SAMUELS,
MAJOR FINLEY, KARL DANIEL
and JOR EL QUINN

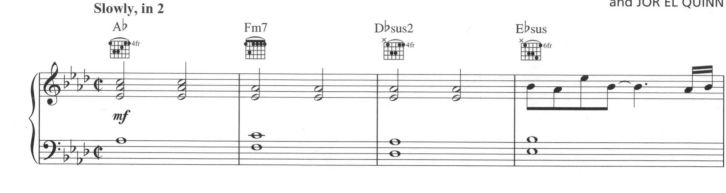

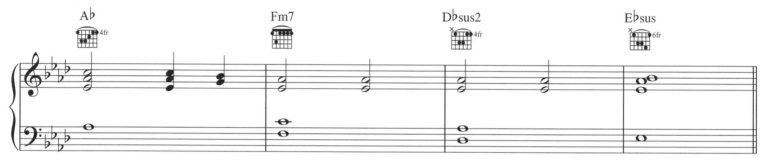

I found love ____ in you,
I found love ____ in you,

and I've learned to love ____ me, ____ too. ____
and no oth - er love ____ will ____ do. ____

YOU & I

Words and Music by JOHN RYAN,
JAMIE SCOTT and JULIAN BUNETTA

Recorded a half step higher.

'Cause you and I... _____

We don't want to be like them, _____ We can make it to ___ the end. _

Noth - ing can come be - tween _ you and ___ I. _____

Not e - ven the gods a - bove _____ can sep - a - rate the two ___ of us. _

WHO YOU LOVE

Words and Music by KATY PERRY
and JOHN MAYER